新华出版社

前　言

故宫,旧称紫禁城。是明、清两代的皇宫,也是我国现存最完整的古建筑群,位于北京市中心。故宫始建于明永乐四年(1406年),永乐十八年(1420年)建成,呈南北向中轴线排列,向两旁展开,南北取直,左右对称。占地面积72万多平方米,屋宇9000余间,建筑面积约15万平方米,周围宫墙长约3公里,四角矗立风格绮丽的角楼。宫墙的四边各有一门,南为午门,东为东华门,西为西华门,北为神武门,墙外有宽52米的护城河环绕,形成一个森严壁垒的城堡。

故宫宫殿的建筑布局有外朝、内廷之分。外朝是皇帝处理朝政、举行各种典礼的地方。从乾清门的横街到午门,主要以太和殿、中和殿、保和殿为中心称前三殿。前三殿两翼东侧的为文华殿,西侧为武英殿。

内廷部分从乾清门开始,包括后三宫(乾清宫、交泰殿、坤宁宫)和御花园;后三宫东面是斋宫、毓庆宫、奉先殿、东六宫,最东是皇极殿、宁寿宫、养性殿、乐寿堂、颐和轩;西面是养心殿、西六宫,最西是慈宁宫、寿安宫等。内廷是皇帝办事、居住和后妃、太后、太妃、皇帝的幼年子女们居住的地方。

故宫整体建筑外观多是红墙、黄瓦、白石栏杆和台阶,在殿堂楼阁,廊房的木结构上,绘有绚丽夺目、金碧辉煌的彩画和其它形式的装饰。虽在明、清时期,多次因火灾局部受毁,屡经重建,至今仍大体保存着初建时的格局和风貌。

故宫以它特殊的魅力闻名于世界,吸引着大批中外游客。我们精选出来的这几十幅图片,意在向广大中外游客呈现那座独具风格的古建筑群的雄伟壮丽,尤其是宫殿中所陈列的珍贵文物,琳琅满目,耐人寻味。同时也表现了我们中华民族悠久的光辉灿烂的文化成就,反映了我国古代劳动人民的高度智慧和创造才能,是祖国珍贵的文化遗产。

Foreword

Called the Purple Forbidden City in the past and located at the centre of Beijing Municipality, the Former Imperial Palace was the imperial palace of Ming and Qing dynasties, and is the existing largest and most perfectly preserved ancient architectural group. The construction project of the Palace began in 1406 (the 4th year of the reign of Yongle, Ming Dynasty), and was completed in 1420 (the 18th year of the same reign). The buildings were arranged symmetrically along an axle and spread to both sides. It occupies an area of over 720000m^2 with over 9000 bays of halls and rooms, the construction area amounts to about 150000m^2, the surrounding walls are about 3 km in length and 4 splendid corner towers stand separately at 4 corners of the city. On the 4 sides of the palace walls, one each gate is open——Wumen at the south, Donghuamen at the east, Xihuamen at the west and Shenumen at the north. A 52-metre-wide moat surrounds outside the walls. Thus the city was made a strongly fortified castle.

The architectural layout of palaces in the Former Imperial Palace can be divided into the outer court and inner court. The former was the palace where emperors handled court affairs and different ceremonies were held. From the east-west street to Wumen, the area centred by Taihe, Zhonghe and Baohe Halls is called the Three Front Halls, and to either sides in front of them, Wenhua Hall and Wuying Hall are on east and west respectively.

The Inner Court is the area inside of Qianqingmen, including the Three Rear Halls (Qianqing, Jiaotai and Kunning) and the Imperial Garden. To the east of the Rear Halls are the Fasting Hall, Yuqing Hall, Fengxian Hall, Eastern Six Halls, and Huangji Hall, Ningshou Hall, Yangxing Hall, Leshou Hall and Yihe Studio are in the eastern end. To the west of the Rear Halls are Yangxin Hall, Western Six Halls, and Cining Hall and Shou'an Hall are at the western end. The inner court was where emperors resided and handled affairs, and where the imperial consorts, empress dowagers, and young children of emperors resided.

The general outside view of architectures in the Former Imperial Palace are red walls, yellow tiles, white marble railings and steps. On the wooden structures of buildings and corridors are painted with dazzlingly gorgeous coloured paintings and decorations in other forms. Though being partly destroyed from fires and repeatedly rebuilt, they still present the original pattern and styles by and large.

The Former Imperial Palace has been well-known all over the world and attracting tremendous amounts of visitors from home and abroad for its special appeals. Here, scores of photos are carefully selected, intending to show visitors about the magnificence of the ancient architectural groups which present unique style, especially about those precious cultural relics displayed in the halls, which are a feast for the eyes and arouse reveries. Showing the long-standing and resplendent cultural achievements attained by the Chinese nation and the superior intelligence and creative talents of ancient Chinese labouring people, they are precious cultural legacies of our Motherland.

まえがき

　昔、「紫禁城」と云う故宮は、北京市の中心に位置して、明と清両代の皇宮で、我国にある一番大きい、または、一番完全に保存された古い建物の群体である。明代の永楽四年(紀元1406年)に建て始め、同十八年(紀元1420年)に作り上げた。建物が、南北中心線にそって排列して、または、両側へ対称に展開している。敷地面積は七十二万平方メートル、建築面積十五万平方メートルで、九千余りの部屋を持っている。その周囲を取り囲んだ塀の長さは三キロメートルで、四隅にはきれい角楼がひとつずつ立ってある。四方の塀に、門がひとつずつあり——南は午門、東は東華門、西は西華門、北は神武門である。幅五十二メートルの外壕が塀の外に取り囲んで、警備が厳重な要塞になっていた。

　故宮は、「外朝」と「内廷」に区別していた。「外朝」は、皇帝が政務を処理するところで、いろいろな礼儀もその場所におこなわれった。乾清門の前にある横町から午門まで、太和殿と中和殿と保和殿を中心として、「前の三殿」とよばれている。その東側に、文華殿、西側に武英殿がある。

　「内廷」は、乾清門から、その中の「後の三宮」(乾清宮、交泰殿、坤寧宮)と御花園を含める。後の三宮の東側は、斎宮、毓慶宮、奉先殿と東六宮がある。一番東のところには、皇極殿、寧寿宮、養性殿、楽寿堂と頤和軒がある。西側には、養心殿と西六宮があり、一番西のところに、慈安宮と寿安宮がある。内廷は、皇帝の住宅で、仕事をするところで、または、皇后、皇妃、太后、太妃と皇帝の若い子供達の住所であった。

　故宮の外観は、主に紅い塀、黄い錬瓦、白玉の欄杆ときざはしが多い。建物の木の構造に、絢繝な彩色画とその他のかざりがある。明代と清代に、いくつ回火事で、ある部分が焼きこわされたが、後に修理されて、いままで、大体もとの姿を見える。

　故宮は、その特別的魅力で、世界に有名になって、おうぜいな客さまを吸いよせていた。このえほんに選択した写真は、おうぜいな客さまへ、あの偉い古いな、特別な風格を持っている建築群とその中に陳列している珍しい文物を紹介しよう意味だ。その珍しい文化財が、我中華民族の絢繝な文化の成果と我国古代労動人民の知恵と創造する才能を反映しているといってもちがいないだろ。

故宮全景
A Panoramic View of the Former Imperial Palace
故宮のパノラマ

太和门广场
The Square in Front of Taihe Gate
太和門の前にある広場

內金水河
Inner Golden Water River
內金水河

午门俯瞰
Looking Down at Wumen
午門を見おろす

铜龟
Bronze Tortoise
銅のかめ

日晷
Sundial
日時計

铜鹤
Bronze Crane
銅のつる

太和殿內景　太和殿俗称金鑾殿。初建于1420年，是故宫最大的建筑。是皇帝举行大典的地方。明朝和清初曾在这里举行殿试。

Inside View of Taihe Hall　Popularly known as Jinluan Hall, Taihe Hall was first built 1420. It is the largest construction in the Former Imperial Palace, and was the place where important ceremonies were held. In Ming and Early Qing Dynasties, court examinations had been held here.

太和殿の内景　太和殿は、俗に金鑾殿と呼ぶ。はじめて、1420年に建てられ、故宫にある一番大きい建物で、昔、皇帝がそこで重要な式典をおこなわすところで、明代と清代に、皇帝が主となっておこなう試験がおこなわったところである。

世宗宪皇帝朝服像　世宗爱新觉罗·胤禛,圣祖第四子。康熙十七年(1678年)十月三十日寅时生于宫内,母孝恭仁皇后。四十五岁继帝位,在位十三年,年号雍正(1723－1735年),雍正十三年八月二十三日死于圆明园,享年五十八岁

A Portrait of Emperor Shizong in Court Costumes

Named Aixin Gioro·Yinzhen, Shizong was the 4th son of Emperor Shengzu. He was born, in the Palace, at the 3.5 A.M. Period on the 30th day of the 10th month in 1678 (the 17th year of the reign of Kangxi, Qing Dynasty. His mother was the Xiao, Gong, Ren Empress. Yinzhen was enthroned when he was 45, ruled for 13 years (1723-1735) under the Title of Yongzheng, and died on the 23rd day of the 8th month of the 13th year of his ruling, when he was 58 years old.

世宗皇帝が大礼服をきていた肖像

　世宗愛新覚羅·胤禛は、聖祖の四番目の子で、1678年(康熙十七年)、旧暦の十月三十日の寅時(午前三時から五時までのころ)に宮の中にうまれ、母親は孝恭仁皇后であった。世宗が、四十五歳に即位して、在位十年、年号は雍正(1723—1735)となり、雍正十三年八月二十三日圓明園に死去し、五十八歳でした。

慈禧像
A Portrait of Cixi
慈禧の肖像

太和殿木雕金漆宝座细部

The Carved Wooden and Gold-painted
Throne in Taihe Hall (Detail)

太和殿にある木彫金漆の帝
座(細部)

矗立在汉白玉台基上的中和殿、保和殿
The Towering Zhonghe Hall and Baohe Hall on Marble Terraces
漢白玉石の基礎の上にそびえている中和殿と保和殿

云龙石雕　位于保和殿和阶陛中间，刻有口衔宝珠的游龙9条，盘旋在山崖、海水和流云图案之中，是明代宫内最大的石雕。清代乾隆年间，又在此石雕上雕刻花纹。

Step Stone Carved with Patterns of Clouds and Dragons
It was located between the ascending steps behind Baohe Hall. Carved with 9 dragons with a pearl in mouth separately which winds among patterns of precipice, the sea and floating clouds, it is the largest stone carving from Ming Dynasty in the Palace. During the reign of Qianlong, Qing Dynasty, more patterns were added to the huge stone.

雲と竜の彫刻をつけた大きい石の飾が、保和殿の段階の真中においていた。九つの竜がそれぞれ、口の中に珠を含んで、海や雲のなかに旋回している図案である。それは、明代て、皇居の中にある一番大きい石彫で、清代の乾隆年間、その上に飾りの模様を増した。

保和殿內景　　原謹身殿。清
代是皇帝阴历年用作宴请王公
贵族和京中文武大臣的场所。

Inside View of Baohe Hall
    It was originally called Jinshen Hall.
In Qing Dynasty, this was the site where
emperors held banquets to entertain
nobilities and high officials and generals
in Beijing.

保和殿の内景　もと、謹身殿
とよばれ、清代では、皇帝が旧
暦の元日に、王公貴族と北京
にいる大臣達を招待
するところである。

太和殿前广场
The Square in Front of Taihe Hall
太和殿の前にある広場

乾清门
Qianqing Gate
乾清門

乾清门前鎏金铜狮
Gold-plated Bronze Lion in Front of Qianqing Gate
乾清門前にある鎏金の銅獅子

乾清宫
Qianqing Palace
乾清宫

乾清宫前鎏金铜亭　又称为江山社稷金殿。金殿上层檐为圆形攒尖，上安宝顶，象征江山社稷、国家政权都掌握在皇帝手中。

Gold-plated Bronze Pavilion in Front of Qianqing Palace
Also called Jingshan Sheji Jindian (the Golden Hall of the Land and Country), it is a pavilion with round and sloping pointed roof topped by a large ball, symbolizing that the country and the state power were controlled by the emperor.

乾清宮の前にある鎏金の銅亭、また、江山社稷金殿ともよばれた。まるくてとがった屋根の上に、まるい「宝頂」がつけられて、社稷と政権はともに皇帝の手中にある。

乾清宮正殿　明代是皇帝的寝宮。清代順治、康熙两帝仍住乾清宮。雍正帝以后，乾清宮改为皇帝处理日常事务的地方。殿内横匾上的"正大光明"四字为顺治帝所写。

The Major Hall of Qianqing Palace
    This was the bedroom of Ming emperors. In Qing Dynasty, Emperors Shunzhi and Kangxi resided here. Beginning from the reign of Yongzheng, the site became where emperors handled daily affairs. The characters on the horizontal plaque, "Zheng Da Guang Ming" ("Just and Honourable") was the inscription of Emperor Shunzhi.

乾清宮の正殿　明代に、これは皇帝の寝室であった。清代の順治皇帝と康熙皇帝がそこに居住していたが、雍正皇帝の時から、乾清宮が皇帝が日常の事務を処理するところとなった。殿の中にある横額のうえにある「正大光明」が、順治皇帝がかいたものだ。

乾清宮雪
A Snow Scene of Qianqing Palace
乾清宮の雪景色

帝后寝宫

Sleeping Room of the Emperor and Empress

皇帝と皇后の寝室

钟表馆內陈列的大自鸣钟　清嘉庆三年（1798年）內务府造办处制造，至今仍在转动。

The Large Chime Clock on Display in the Hall of Clocks and Watches
    Produced 1798 (the 3rd year of the reign of Jiaqing, Qing Dynasty) by Zhi Ban Chu (the Office of Productions) under Nei Wu Fu(the Office of Domestic Affairs), it is still working now.

時計陳列室にある大きい時報時計は、清代嘉慶三年(1798年)内務府の造弁処でこしらえたもので、いまでもよくうぐいている。

养心殿正间　是"工"字形的宫殿。清代皇帝经常在这里召见大臣、引见官员，有时也在这里接见外国使臣。康熙五十九年（1720年）十二月，康熙皇帝在这里接见罗马教皇使臣嘉乐。

The Major Room of Yangxin Hall
　　The Hall is an I-shaped construction. In this room, emperors of Qing Dynasty used to give audiences to high officials and sometimes foreign diplomatic delegates. In 1720 (the 12th month of the 59th year of the reign of Kangxi), the Emperor gave audience to the envoy of the Pope of Roma.

養心殿の正殿は、I形の建物である。清代の皇帝が、そこで大臣を召見しながら、外国の使臣と面会することもあった。康熙皇帝は、1720年にこのところでローマ法皇の使臣を引見した。

坤宁宫东暖阁　是皇帝大婚的洞房。
Eastern Cabinet of Kunning Palace, the Bridal Chamber of Emperors
坤寧宮の東暖閣は、皇帝の結婚するときの洞房である。

故宮三大殿鳥瞰
A Bird's-eye View of the 3 Great Hall in the Former Imperial Palace
故宮三大殿の鳥瞰

坤宁门雪
Snow Scene of Kunning Palace
坤寧門の雪景色

远眺乾隆花园
A Distant View of the Qianlong Garden
遠いところから乾隆花園を眺める

养性斋　是一座凹字形二层小楼，宣统皇帝溥仪退位以后，曾聘请教师在这里学习英语、数学。

Yangxingzhai Studio　A U-shaped 2-storeyed Petit Building Where Pu Yi (the Abdicated Emperor Xuantong) Learned English and Mathimatics.

養性斎は、U形の二階建ビールである。宣統皇帝溥儀が退位したあとに、ここで先生から英語と数学をならいしたことがあった。

御花园春 御花园原名宫后苑,建于明永乐年间,东西长130米,南北宽90米,面积11700平方米。

A Scene of the Imperial Garden in Spring Originally called Gong Hou Yuan (Garden in the Rear Court), it was built during the reign of Yongle, Ming Dynasty. Being 130-metre long from east to west, and 90-metre wide, it occupies an area of 11700 metre square.

御花園は、もと「宮の後苑」とよばれ、明代永楽年間に建てられ、東—西の長さは130メートル、南—北ノ幅は90メートルで、面積は11700平方メートルである。

御花园一角
A Corner of the Imperial Garden
御花園の一隅

御花园雪
Snow Scene of the Imperial Garden
御花園の雪景色

千秋亭
Qianqiu Pavilion

千秋亭

天一门——连理树
Lianli Tree in Tianyi Gate
天一門——連理樹

养心门
Yangxin Gate
養心門

养心门前鎏金铜狮
Gold-plated Bronze Lion in Front of
Yangxin Gate
養心門のまえにある金つけた
銅の獅子

坤宁宫洞房喜床外侧挂的"五彩百子帐"。

The "Multi-coloured 100-male-baby Curtain" Hang at the Outer Side of the Wedlock Bed in Kunning Palace

坤寧宮洞房寝台の外側にかけている「五彩百子帳」

储秀宫宝石
Diamond in Chuxiu Palace
储秀宮にある宝石

储秀宫 是明、清两代后妃居住的宫室。西太后（即慈禧太后）刚进宫被封为兰贵人时曾在这里居住。

Chuxiu Palace was the residence of imperial consorts in Ming and Qing Dynasties. Cixi had lived here when she was chosen into the Palace and made the "Lan Guiren" (Guiren being a female official in the palace).

儲秀宮は、明代と清代に、皇后と皇妃が住る宮室である。慈禧がはじめて「蘭貴人」に封じたころ、ここに住った。

皇帝批阅的奏摺和使用的文房四宝
Memorandum Viewed, and Writing Utensils used, by the Emperor
皇帝が批判を加えた上奏文とつかった文房具

长春宫皇后寝室
The Bedroom of the Empress in Changchun Palace
長春宮にある皇后の寝室

皇后宝座
The Throne of the Empress
皇后の宝座

长春宫妃嫔寝室

The Bedroom of Imperial Concubine in Changchun Palace

長春宮、妃嬪の寝室

雨花阁　內供西天梵王像。是西藏喇嘛为皇帝唪经祝福之所。

Yuhua Cabinet　With enshrined portrait of King of the Western Paradise, this was the place where Tibetan Lamas incanted texts blessing the emperor.

雨花閣は、西天梵王を供えてある、西蔵喇嘛が読経して、皇帝のために祝福するところである。

九龙壁
Nine-Dragon Screen
九竜壁

招丝景泰蓝佛手

Filigree Cloisonné Buddha's-hand

七宝焼の仏手柑

远眺宁寿门
A Distant View of Ningshou Gate
とおいところから寧寿門を眺める。

皇极殿
Huangji Hall

皇極殿

金佛塔 通高92cm，底面50cm×50cm。塔顶、塔身、龛门周围以及坛城、塔的下边，遍嵌红、蓝宝石、珍珠、绿松石等各式宝石，华贵而庄严。

Gold Buddha Pagoda It is 92cm high, with a 50cm×50cm bottom. Rubies, sapphires, pearls and turquoises are inlaid all through the Pagoda and the niche, looking luxurious and solemn.

金の仏塔 高さは92cm、底の面積は50cm×50cm、体じゅ珠宝が象嵌されて、派手で荘厳な優良品である。

养性门
Yangxing Gate
養性門

养性殿藻井
Caisson Ceiling in Yangxing Hall
養性殿の模様を描いた天井

寿山（玉雕）
"Mountain of Longevity" (A Jade
Carving)
寿山(玉石の彫刻)

青玉《大禹治水图》高2.24米,宽0.96米,重约5300多公斤,是整块碧玉雕琢而成。

"Emperor Yu Regulating Rivers and Watercourses" (A Sapphire Carving)
2.24m high, 0.96m wide and about 5300 kg in weight, it was carved out from a single piece of sapphire.

サファイア彫刻《大禹治水図》 高さ2.24メートル、幅0.96メートル、重さ5300キロ位で、ひとつままの碧玉で彫刻されたものである。

金瓯永固杯　通高12.5cm，口径8cm，足高5cm，此杯为清朝皇帝每年正月初一举行开笔仪式时的专用酒杯，系清帝世袭之物。取名"金瓯永固"，寓意大清皇权巩固，长治久安。

"Jin Ou Yong Gu" Cup
12.5cm high, 8cm in diameter at the mouth, 5cm high at the foot, this was a special wine cup handed down in the imperial household, which emperors used when the ceremonies for starting the use of the brushes were held on the Lunar New Year's Day. The name of the cup implied that the imperial power would last forever.

「金瓯永固」のコップ　高さ12.5cm、口径8cm、足の高さ5cm、清代皇室の代代受け継ぐもので、皇帝が毎年正月の元旦に執務が始まる儀式につかおコップである。その名前は、「皇権は強固で、永くに継ぐ」意味である。

清代皇帝所用宝玺甚多, 大部分为玉质, 此为金质 "天子之宝"。

Many were the imperial seals used by emperors of Qing Dynasty, and most of them were carved out from jade. This is a gold seal carved with "Seal of the Son of Heaven"

清代皇帝の印章が多い、大部分は玉印である。これは金の「天子之宝」印章である。

皇后玉印

The other one is a jade seal of the empress

皇后の玉印

太和殿景泰藍象身香炉

An Incense Burner in the Shape of An
Elephant, which is in Taihe Hall

太和殿にある景泰藍の象形の
香炉

御袍局部
Imperial Robe (Detail)
竜袍(局部)

缂丝椅披
Chair Drape Made of Tapestry of Cut Silk
刻系の椅子のカバー

故宮俯瞰
A Panoramic View of the Former Imperial Palace
空から見た故宮

远眺太和门
A Distant View of Taihe Gate
遠いところから太和門を眺める。

明·万历孝端皇后的嵌珠宝点翠凤冠
The Phoenix Crown Inlaid with Jewelries of Empress Xiaoduan of Emperor Wanli, Ming Dynasty
明代万暦皇后の珠玉宝石象嵌した鳳冠

清代凤冠是清晚期皇后的夏朝
冠

The Phoenix Crown of Later Qing
Empresses

晚清皇后の鳳冠

梳妆用具
Make-up Utensils
化粧する用具

天球仪　清乾隆年间由宫中造
办处制造。用黄金作球体，珍珠
镶嵌成星座，北极有时辰盘，球
下面安指南针。

Celestial Globe　Produced by Office of
Productions in the Palace during the
reign of Qianlong, Qing Dynasty, it was a
gold ball inlaid with pearls as
constellations. On the north pole is a
plate of hour-periods, and a compass is
set under the ball.

天体儀　清代乾隆年間造弁処
でこしらえ、黄金の球体
のうえに、珍珠を象嵌して、星
座となっている。北極
のところに時辰盤がある。球の
下に羅針盤がつけている。

故宫内收藏的明·嘉靖年间的
书画珍品

Treasure of Calligraphy,
and Painting fram theReign
of Jiajing, Ming Dynasty,

Which was Colleeted by the
Former Imperial Palace

故宫に収集した明代嘉靖年間
の書道と画の上等品

清·郑燮"墨竹轴"

A Painting Scroll of Mozhu Bamboo
by Zheng Xie, Qing Dynasty Calligraphy
and Painting Treasures of the Reign of

Jiajing, Ming Dynasty, in the Former
Imperial Palace.

清代鄭燮の「墨竹軸」

皇帝休息室
The Lounge for the Emperor
皇帝の休息室

招丝景泰蓝双龙
Filigree Cloisonné Double Dragons
景泰藍の双竜

明·嘉靖五彩鱼藻瓷罐
Multi-coloured Porcelain Jar with Patterns of Fish and Waterweeds (The. Reign of Jiajing, Ming Dynasty)
明代嘉靖年間五彩の魚と藻の 模様がつけていた磁碗

乾隆・粉彩描金海晏河清瓷尊

Famille Rose and Gold-traced Porcelain
Vase with the Painting Peaceful Sea
and Limpid River (the Reign of
Qianlong Qing Dynasty)

乾隆年間の粉彩描金「海晏河
清」磁瓶

故宫俯瞰全貌
A Panoramic View of the Former Imperial Palace
故宫の全貌

故宫——景山黄昏
The Former Imperial Palace and Jingshan at Dusk
故宫——景山の日暮れ時

太和殿雪景
Snow Scene of Taihe Hall
太和殿の雪景色

清・康熙黃地珐琅彩花卉瓷碗
Yellow Porcelain Bowl with coloured Flower Patterns (the Reign of Kangxi Qing Dynasty)
清代康熙年代の彩色花模様をつけた黄色磁碗

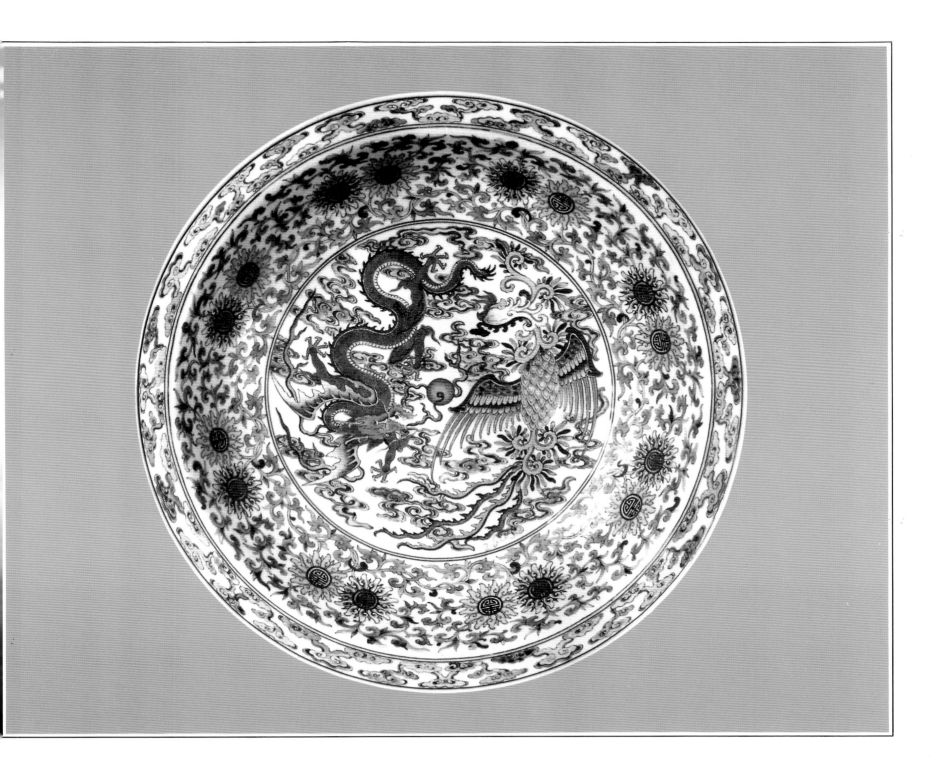

龙凤瓷盘

Porcelain Plate with the Pattern of Dragon and Phoenix

竜鳳模様の磁盤

雕漆龙舟盘

Carved Lacquer Plate with the Pattern of Dragon Boat

彫漆の竜舟模様がつけた盤

畅音阁是故宫内最大的一座戏台,建于乾隆年间,每逢时节和皇帝生日,帝后都在这里看戏。

Changyin Cabinet It is the largest stage in the Former Imperial Palace, which was built during the reign of Qianlong. In festivals and birthdays of emperors, the emperor and empress would come and enjoy dramas here

暢音閣は、故宮にある芝居の舞台の中で一番大きいもので、乾隆年間建てられ、祭日と皇帝の誕辰日に、皇帝と皇后がここで芝居を見た。

故宫门窗雕刻二龙戏珠局部
Door and Window Carved with the
Pattern of Dragon in the Former Imperial
Palace (Detail)
故宮の戸とまどに彫刻した竜(局部)

珍妃井引起游客兴趣
Zhenfei Well attracts tourists.
珍妃井が客さまの興味をおこされている

宁寿宫西夹道
Passageway at the West Side of Ningshou Palace
寧寿宮西の通道

順贞门
Shunzhen Gate
順貞門

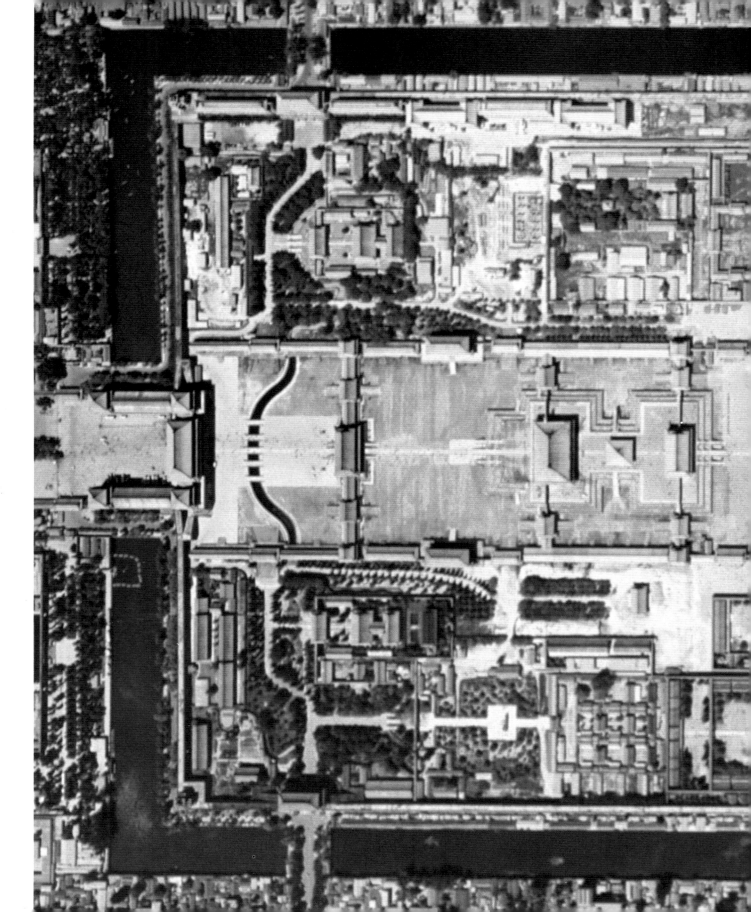

故宫鸟瞰
Bird's-eye View of the Former
Imperial Palace
故宮の鳥瞰

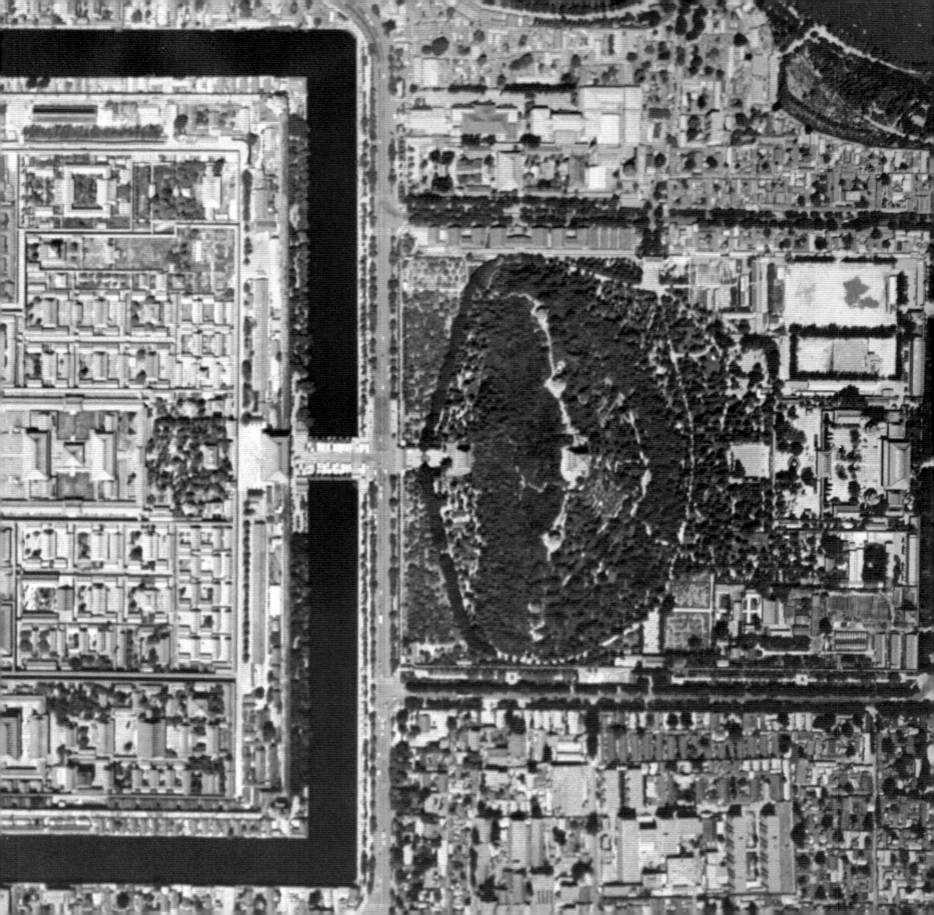

角楼春色
A Corner Tower in Spring
角楼の春景色

角楼黄昏

A Corner Tower at Dusk

角楼の日暮れ時

东北角角楼远眺

A Distant View of the Corner Tower at the Northeastern Corner

遠いところから東北かどの角楼を眺める。

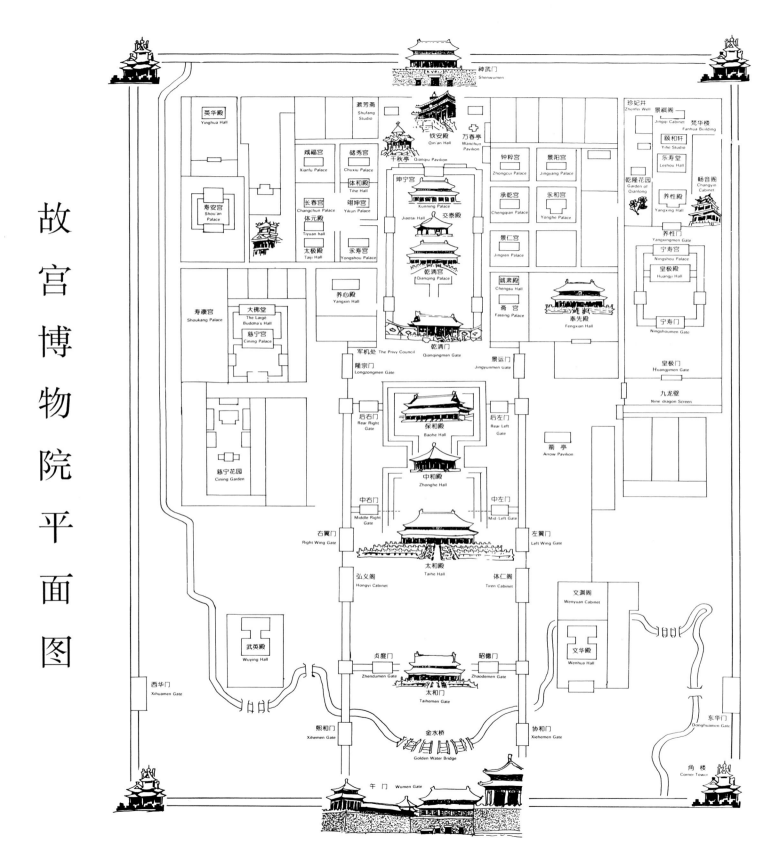

故宫博物院平面图

顾　　问：穆青　石少华　杨牧之
编委主任：许邦　阎振国　张万舒
编辑委员：（按性氏笔画为序）
　　　　　牛嵩林　卞志武　甘纯庚　何世尧
　　　　　邵柏林　周　毅　茹遂初　柳成行
　　　　　胡维标　陈　勃　陈长芬　鄂　毅
　　　　　冯法光　程克雄　杨春华　熊迪强
　　　　　刘　军　刘　毅　刘世昭
特邀编委：刘连芳　张文广
主　　编：杨春华　冯法光
特邀执行编辑：胡维标
责任编辑：徐文金　李　红　陈卫东
翻　　译：麦仰曾
装帧设计：胡维标　李　红
书名题字：徐楚德
摄　　影：胡维标　白雏虎　谷维恒　杨　茵
　　　　　鄂　毅　张承志　王文波　顾　公
　　　　　常胜凯　华　瑛　昊　霞　董维东

Consultants: Mu Qing　Shi Shaohua　Yang Muzhi
Directors of the Editorial Board:
　　　Xu Bang　　Yan Zhenguo　　Zhang Wanshu
Members of the Editorial Board:
　　　Niu Songlin　　Bian Zhiwu　　Gan Chungeng
　　　He Shiyao　　Shao Bailin　　Zhou Yi
　　　Ru Suichu　　Liu Chenghang　Hu Weibiao
　　　Chen Bo　　Chen Changfen　E Yi
　　　Feng Faguang　Cheng Kexiong　Yang Chunhua
　　　Xiong Diqiang　Liu Jun　　　Liu Yi
　　　Liu Shizhao
Specially Invited Editors: Liu Lianfang　Zhang Wenguang
Chief Editors: Yang Chunhua　Feng Faguang
Executive Editor: Hu Weibiao

Editors in Charge: Xu Wenjin　Li Hong　Chen Weidong
Translator: Mai Yangzeng
Binding Designers: Hu Weibiao　Li Hong
Title Inscription by Xu Chude

Photograhers:
　　Hu Weibiao　　Bai Chuhu　　Gu Weiheng
　　Yang Yin　　　E Yi　　　　Zhang Chengzhi
　　Wang Wenbo　　Gu Gong　　Chang Shengkai
　　Hua Ying　　　Hao Xia　　Dong Weidong

顧問：穆　青　石少華　楊牧之
主任編集委員：許　邦　閻振国　張万舒
編集委員(姓氏順)：
　牛嵩林　卞志武　甘純庚　何世尭
　邵柏林　周　毅　茹遂初　柳成行
　胡維標　陳　勃　陳長芬　鄂　毅
　馮法光　程克雄　楊春華　熊迪強
　劉　军　劉　毅　劉世昭
特別招請編集委員：劉連芳　張文広
編集主任：楊春華　馮法光
特別招請執行編集人：胡維標
責任編集人：徐文金　李　紅　陳衛東
翻　訳：麦仰曽
装丁設計人：胡維標　李　紅
書名題字：徐楚德

故　宮

新　华　出　版　社　出　版　发　行
北　京　利　丰　雅　高　长　城　印　刷
有　限　公　司　制　版　印　刷
1996年2月第一版第一次印刷
787×1092　　12开　　8印张
ISBN 7-5011-3031-0/J・139

005000